What exactly is t
whose letters and
equally large spa

The principle of
its aesthetics fa
"Mono Moment" tra
aesthetic and gives insight into the world
of monospaced fonts.

Content

4   Content

6   Intro

12   Typefaces

1955-1997

42   Talk 1

Horst Wöhrle

44   Typefaces

2001-2009

70   Talk 2

María Ramos

74   Typefaces

2010-2016

Content

122	Talk 3
	André Leonhardt
	Dennis Michaelis

128	Typefaces
	2010-2020

176	Talk 4
	Marcus Sterz

180	Typefaces
	2020

190	Index

198	Appendix

204	Imprint

Intro

Friedrich Nietzsche was probably one of the first to feel the aesthetic appeal of monospaced typefaces. Since he started writing with a typewriter, typefaces, and punctuation have been important to him. In the meantime, we encounter monospaced typefaces regularly in everyday life: in design and in art, in coding, on tax records, or on our ID. If you take a closer look, you will encounter non-proportional typefaces more often than expected.

Monospaced typefaces are defined by their fixed, equal width for all characters. Every character, letter, and number occupies horizontally and vertically the same space. Proportional typefaces, in turn, have harmoniously balanced spaces with variable widths between their characters. The widths are not set proportional. That is why monospaced typefaces are also named non-proportional.

What exactly is the attraction of typefaces, whose letters and characters each occupy an equally large space?

Emil Ruderer, for sure one of the most notable typographers of the last century, attributes the appearance of typewriter typefaces to an international character. "International" also stands for "generally valid" or "universal." The design of a universal, generally valid typeface appears withdrawn. The typeface does not seem strongly designed. The aesthetic impact of monospaced typefaces has often been described as "faceless" or "neutral."

The relationship between the characters and space deposits significantly from other typefaces. Despite their high recognition value, monospaced typefaces enable designers to present content factual and prosaic, without being influenced by the design of the typeface. Thus, the character of the typeface is characterized by its high aesthetic intrinsic value. The phenomenon of a characterless typeface occurs, which is nevertheless full of character.

The character of monospaced typefaces distinguishes itself by the effect of the entire typeface rather than by a single letter. It is therefore initially defined by the strict positioning of each character and the resulting restrictions, or certain "basic rules" when designing it. By using a fixed space for each character an enigmatic typeface is created. It maintains rhythm and freedom. The design restrictions also define the aesthetics.

How did such a typeface character originate and what was the genesis of monospaced writing?

The birth of non-proportional typefaces is heralded by the concise rattling and squiggling of the line feed when typing on the typewriter. Monospaced typefaces were created due to the technical characteristics of the typewriter. Such and similar instruments exist since the 19th century. They established themselves at the time of the "technological typographic revolution" in the following century. The typewriter thus joins the inventions of the Linotype typesetting machine, the offset printing process or the photo typesetting process and revolutionizes writing.

Years ago everyone was familiar with the formal design of monospaced typefaces from everyday correspondence. Until then, the attraction was mainly based on the technical innovations caused by the typewriter. At this moment, it is less the aesthetics of the typeface that inspires, more the speed of writing, the ability to print a large amount of text in a short time, and to reproduce it, if necessary.

The possibility of word processing and typesetting with using the computer marked a turning point for typefaces and the handling of it. In order to write texts, nobody is bound to the typewriter anymore. Nowadays non-designers and designers can choose out of a countless number of typefaces.

The rules in the design, which were once dictated by the technical limitations of the typewriter, do not only invite to experiment. The optically screened arrangement of the letters benefits text and illustrations, in which each individual sign is meaningful and distinguishable. With their clear design language, monospaced fonts find a new purpose in digital applications. Due to the clear aesthetics, the fonts in coding programs are almost exclusively monospaced.

In a communication environment in which people are mainly surrounded by proportional typefaces such as *Arial, Helvetica*, or *Times New Roman*, monospaced typefaces appear kind of special and rare in correspondence. This allows the reader to have a more personal reference to what is written. As a result, in a world longing for individuality, monospaced typefaces find more influence again.

Due to the increase in typeface production over the past
few decades, almost every well-developed font family also
has a mono or semi-mono cut. When searching for the word
"monospace" on the World Wide Web, countless entries can
be found in addition to the results such as "I am looking for a
beautiful monospaced font," "Top Ten Monospace Fonts," or
"Best Monospace Fonts for Coding." At a moment when it has
never been easier to design and publish typefaces, there is a
great deal of confusion.

The principle of monospaced typeface and its aesthetics fascinates and polarizes. *Mono Moment* tracks down the
euphoria for an aesthetic and give an insight into the world
of monospaced typefaces. It is an opportunity to discover
monospaced typefaces bundled up. Thus, the magazine is
not only aimed at type designers and fanatics, typographers
and designers, but also at people who are interested in typefaces or who get touched or fascinated by it. It can therefore
serve as a work of reference for those who have discovered
the fascination monospace.

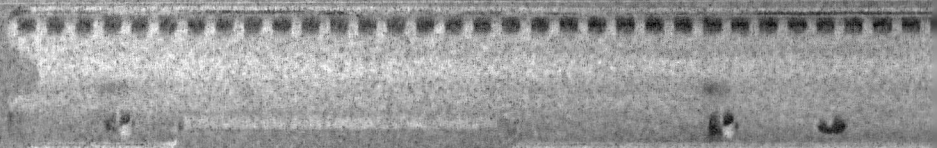

Typefaces

Courier

Lowercase	abcdefghijklmnopqrstuvwxyz

Uppercase	ABCDEFGHIJKLMNOPQRSTUVWXYZ

Punctuation	. , : ; - — — _ ! ? ¡ … • • * + ' " " ' ` ´ ‹ « » ›

Symbols	§©®℗™ FAXSMTEL £ @ &

Ligatures	ff fi fl

Figures	1234567890

Designer	Howard Kettler

Foundry	IBM

Release	1955

World Wide Web

"A letter can be just
an ordinary messenger,
or it can be the
courier, which radiates
dignity, prestige, and
stability."

Howard Kettler

Have a look at all the other versions
of "Courier." You can discover
"Courier New," "Courier Screenplay,"
"Dark Courier," and more.

Designed by Howard Kettler
of IBM as a typewriter
typeface. Originally re-
leased as "Messenger."
Later redrawn with Adrian
Frutiger as "Courier New"
for the IBM Selectric
Composer.[1]

Pica 10 Pitch

Lowercase

abcdefghijklmnopqrstuvwxyz

Uppercase

ABCDEFGHIJKLMNOPQRSTUVWXYZ

Punctuation

. , : ; - — — _ ! ? ¡ … · · * + ' " " ' ` ´ ‹ « » ›

Symbols

§ © ® ™ ¶ £ @ &

Ligatures

fi   fl

Figures

1234567890

Designer

IBM

Foundry

Linotype

World Wide Web

192 pt

AeQ

```
                    This Page Prepared With
                    PICA (10 pitch) Spacing

                   IBM "SELECTRIC" TYPE SAMPLES
```

COURIER	Similar to Courier Type offered with the IBM Standard Typewriter, this style is a popular choice for many typing applications. 1234567890.
MANIFOLD	FOR INVOICING, BILLING AND A WIDE RANGE OF FORMS, A LARGE SANS-SERIF STYLE THAT PRODUCES A LARGE NUMBER OF CARBON COPIES. 1234567890.
PICA	For general use in a wide range of applications. De-signed to blend well with the Pica style of the IBM Standard Typewriter. 1234567890.
DELEGATE	To convey the feeling of printed material. A weighted type recommended for test copy, or for correspondence, where preferred. 1234567890.
ADVOCATE	For reports, stencils, offset and spirit processes, as well as routine correspondence. A square-serif face for a modern look. 1234567890.
LETTER GOTHIC	This sans-serif style looks well with 10 or 12 pitch. Recommended for general correspondence and statistical reports. 1234567890.
LIGHT ITALIC	A change of pace typestyle that may be used singly or in combination with other typestyles to add impact to correspondence, reports and memos. 1234567890.
PRESTIGE ELITE	For reports, spirit hektograph and photo-offset appli-cations. Correspondence is attractive, too, when typed in this functional Elite type. 1234567890.
ELITE	For general use in a wide range of applications. De-signed to blend well with the Elite typestyle of the IBM Standard Typewriter. 1234567890.
SCRIPT	For a warm, personal touch in correspondence. The simulated handwriting also provides effective change of pace in memos, bulletins or flyers. 1234567890.
ADJUTANT	To convey the feeling of printed material. A weighted type recommended for text copy or for correspondence where it is preferred. 1234567890.
SCRIBE	For reports, manifolding, stencils, spirit hektograph and offset applications. A stylized square-serif also distinct for correspondence. 1234567890.
DUAL GOTHIC	This sans-serif type similar to Dual Basic of the IBM Standard Typewriter has crisp, sharp appearance which adds to legibility. 1234567890.
UNIVERSAL SYMBOL	γδεθτυξιορπασφιληʃκω¨±ζχψ×δνμ´¯₍⁄│{}±⌐⌠⌡∫_⌐Γ∆÷θ→ ΤΣ↑↓ΛΠVΣΦ<Λ¶>§Ω^·=Ξ¥∝∞√ə¯÷∫1234567890

"Efficiency is More Demanding"
IBM Selectric typewriter type samples. Included in an
undated IBM promotional booklet / folder for Selectric
typewriters.

A typeface designed for
the "IBM Standard and
Selectric typewriters."
Revived by "Bitstream"
(as Pica 10 Pitch) in 1990.

Letter Gothic

Lowercase

abcdefghijklmnopqrstuvwxyz

Uppercase

ABCDEFGHIJKLMNOPQRSTUVWXYZ

Punctuation

. , : ; - – — _ ! ? ¡ … • · *+ ' " " ' ` ´ ‹ « » ›

Ligatures

fi fl

Figures

1234567890

Designer	Roger Roberson
Foundry	IBM
Release	1962
World Wide Web	

164 pt

I x G

"Letter Gothic" was designed by Roger Roberson for IBM sometime between 1956 and 1962. Point of Inspiration was the typeface "Optima." A monospaced sans-serif font designed for use on an IBM Selectric typewriter.[2]

	a	b	c	d
A	100 000 000	90	600 000 000	0
B	10 000 000	900	60 000 000	0
C	1000 000	9 000	6000 000	0
D	100 000	90 000	600 000	0
E	10 000	900 000	60 000	0
F	1 000	9000 000	6 000	0
G	100	90 000 000	600	0
H	10	900 000 000	60	0

AO Mono

Lowercase

abcdefghijklmnopqrstuvwxyz

Uppercase

ABCDEFGHIJKLMNOPQRSTUVWXYZ

Punctuation

. , : ; - - — _ ! ? . . * + " „ ' ‹ « » ›

Symbols

§0@&€$

Figures

1234567890

Atelier Olschinsky

148 pt

FiQ

Orator

Lowercase

A B C D E F G H I J K L M N O P Q R S T U V W X Y Z

Uppercase

A B C D E F G H I J K L M N O P Q R S T U V W X Y Z

Punctuation

. , : ; - – — _ ! ? ¡ … • * + ' " " ' ` ´ ‹ « » ›

Symbols

§ © ® ™ ¶ £ @ &

Figures

1 2 3 4 5 6 7 8 9 0

Designer	JOHN SCHEPPLER
Foundry	ADOBE ORIGINALS
Release	1962
World Wide Web	

170 pt

MKB

"ORATOR" IS A MONOSPACED TYPEFACE MADE UP OF
CAPITALS AND SMALL CAPITALS ONLY. IT CAN BE
USED FOR TABULAR MATERIAL OR TECHNICAL DOCUMEN-
TATION. THE NAME "ORATOR" COMES FROM THE NOTION
THAT CAPITALS AND SMALL CAPITALS ARE CLEARER
THAN UPPER AND LOWERCASE LETTERS, THUS MAKING
IT USEFUL FOR SPEECH NOTES. IT WAS DESIGNED FOR
IBM TYPEWRITERS BY JOHN SCHEPPLER.[3]

8 pt	DESIGNED FOR IBM TYPEWRITERS
9 pt	DESIGNED FOR IBM TYPEWRITERS
10 pt	DESIGNED FOR IBM TYPEWRITERS
11 pt	DESIGNED FOR IBM TYPEWRITERS
12 pt	DESIGNED FOR IBM TYPEWRITERS
14 pt	DESIGNED FOR IBM TYPEWRITERS
18 pt	DESIGNED FOR IBM TYPEWRITERS
24 pt	DESIGNED FOR IBM TYPE
30pt	DESIGNED FOR IBM T
36 pt	DESIGNED FOR I
48 pt	DESIGNED FO
60 pt	DESIGNED
72 pt	DESIGNE

platelet

Lowercase

abcdefghijklmnopqrstuvwxyz

Uppercase

ABCDEFGHIJKLMNOPQRSTUVWXYZ

Punctuation

., : ; - – — _ ! ? ¡ . … • · * + ' " " ' ' ‹ « » ›

Symbols

§ © ® ™ ¶ £ € @ &

Ligatures

fi fl

Figures

1234567890

Designer	conor mangat

Foundry	emigre

Release	1993

World Wide Web	

256 pt

PWF

The inspiration for "plate-let" came from the california license plate. similar to the composing restrictions of the typewriter, the manufacture of license plates also requires the use of monospaced type; not only for mechanical requirements, but also to fulfill the need of fitting a fixed number of characters onto each plate while maximizing their legibility at a distance.

platelet contains some unexpected solutions to the various problems facing monospaced designs. it also offers solutions that address the reduced legibility of geometric designs, which have a tendency to render many characters indistinguishable, thus reducing their function for text applications.

the "m" and "w" cleverly solve the density problem of the three stems by shortening the middle one. the "i" and "l" fill their width not with the standard extended serifs, but with a large curved lead-out stroke.

another creative solution is the lowercase "b," which incorporates the upper case form within the lower case character. this increases the recognition factor of the "b," which would otherwise be very similar to other characters, such as the "d," due to the geometric rigidity of platelet's letter form construction.[4]

x		a	
	w		g
		●	
	g		
		ƀ	
ε			

TheSans Mono

Lowercase

abcdefghijklmnopqrstuvwxyz

Uppercase

ABCDEFGHIJKLMNOPQRSTUVWXYZ

Punctuation

. , : ; - – — _ ! ? ¡ … • · * + ' "" ' ` ´ ‹ « » ›

Symbols

§©®™¶£€@&←↑→↓↖↗↘↙■💡

Ligatures

fi

Figures

1234567890

1234567890

Designer	Lucas de Groot
Foundry	LucasFonts
Release	1994
World Wide Web	
176 pt	EqN

Andalé Mono

Lowercase

abcdefghijklmnopqrstuvwxyz

Uppercase

ABCDEFGHIJKLMNOPQRSTUVWXYZ

Punctuation

. , : ; - – — _ ! ? ¡ … • · * + ' " " ' ` ´ ‹ « » ›

Symbols

§©®™¶£@&☺☻☼♀♂♠♣♥♦♪♫

Ligatures

fi fl

Figures

1234567890

Designer	Steve Matteson
Foundry	Monotype
Release	1995
World Wide Web	

About

Andalé Mono is a monospaced sans-serif typeface designed by Steve Matteson in 1995. It was designed to be a highly-legible font for programming usage. *Andalé Mono* used to be bundled with Microsoft Windows, but has since been replaced by *Lucida Console*.[6]

172 pt

YmI

Base Mono

abcdefghijklmnopqrstuvwxyz

abcdefghijklmnopqrstuvwxyz

Uppercase

ABCDEFGHIJKLMNOPQRSTUVWXYZ

ABCDEFGHIJKLMNOPQRSTUVWXYZ

Punctuation

. , : ; - – — _ ! ? ¡ … • · * + ' " " ' ` ´ ‹ « » ›

. , : ; - – — _ ! ? ¡ … • · * + ' " " ' ` ´ ‹ « » ›

Symbols

§©®™¶£@&

§©®™¶£@&

Ligatures

fifl

fi fl

Figures

1234567890

1234567890

Designer	Zuzana Licko

Foundry	Emigre

Release	1997

World Wide Web

159 pt

WrB

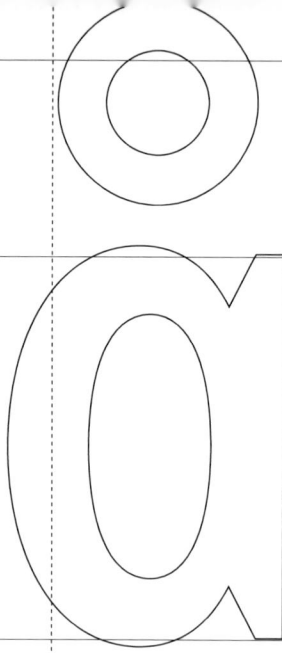

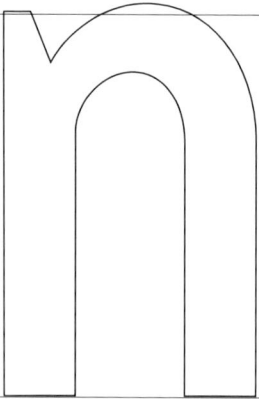

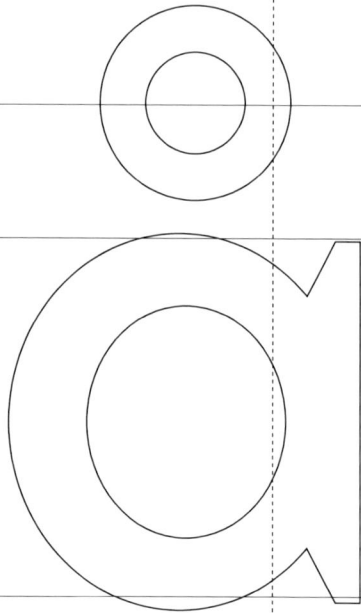

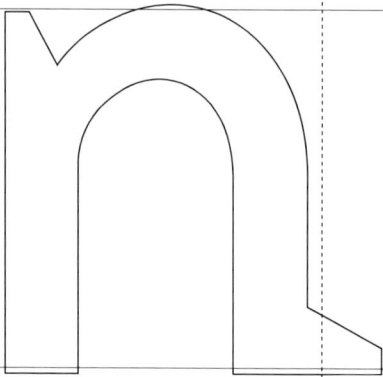

"Base Mono," as its name implies, belongs to a category of typefaces characterized by letter designs
that each occupy a single set width, like the infa-
mous typewriter font "Courier" (designed in 1956 by
Howard Kettler), and the many other monospaced fonts
that inspired its design.

Monospaced typefaces live on the "vernacular" side
of legibility. When set in text, they do not gener-
ate a silky smooth image on the page. The "i," "l,"
and "j" usually float in their spaces, while the "m"
and "w" are squeezed in, creating a somewhat jarring
text image.

Still, monospaced typefaces might have a leg up in
the legibility department. Since the typewriter was
an affordable and easy to use typesetting tool, it
rapidly became the standard for academic, business,
and legal writing, and for formal and informal correspondence. Despite its aesthetic handicaps, it was
able to establish a look and feel that became ac-
cepted as a highly functional means of communication
all over the world. If it is true that people read
best what they read most, then monospaced type must
contain plenty of features worth considering when
exploring legibility.[7]

First of all, monospace typefaces are an involuntarily imperfect result of a time-specific technology.

The invention of the typewriter at the end of the 19th century (in 1873 the American company "Remington" acquired the patent from the developers "Sholes," "Glidden," and "Soule") shaped the development of many decades. From today's perspective, the astonishingly "simple" mechanics of the type-lever-devices also worked so well because of the reduction in the letter width to just one. Last but not least, the fact that an "l" or an "i" should be as wide as an "m" was a decision of aesthetics – Gutenberg went the opposite way when he invented lead type-setting and letterpress around 1450 and produced frequently occurring letters like the small "e" in several different widths, only to make it easier to set the lines in justification at the time. Two worlds, two systems …

At the time the mechanical typewriter was being developed, so called Egyptienne typefaces, i.e. serif-emphasized Linear Antiqua typefaces, were in fashion. The emphasized serifs eased the stylistic difficulty of bringing the letters to the same level. Hence typewriter typefaces were originally all Egyptienne fonts.

The idea that the form follows the function so logically compelling had an attractive charm for purists among the applied and free artists. No wonder that art-enunciations (collages, visual poetry, conceptual art, etc.), who subsequently worked with text and writing, liked to use typewriter typefaces. The conscious application of this typeface with its very own aesthetics was and is program: praise of reduction.

Horst Wöhrle

Eureka Mono

Lowercase	a b c d e f g h i j k l m n o p q r s t u v w x y z

Uppercase	A B C D E F G H I J K L M N O P Q R S T U V W X Y Z

Punctuation	. , : ; - – — _ ! ? ¡ … • · * + ' " " ' ` ´ ‹ « » ›

Symbols	§ © ® ™ ¶ £ @ &

Ligatures	fi fl

Figures	1 2 3 4 5 6 7 8 9 0

Designer	Peter Bil'ak
Foundry	FontFont
Release	2001
World Wide Web	

205 pt

GeK

"It is the white space that
we unconsciously read, not
the actual letterforms.
Looser spacing helps to
avoid the typographic noise
inside a text, and retains
the individuality of the
letters."

Peter Bil'ak

The first drawings of "Eureka" date from 1995 when it was designed for the bilingual text "Transparency." The typeface works particularly well with languages that commonly use accented characters. Because most contemporary Latin typefaces have large x-heights, little room is left to accommodate the accents which end up being small and tightly wedged in place.

In 1997, "Eureka" was recognized at the National Design Award competition organized by the Slovak Design Center. At the 19th International Biennale of Graphic Design during the year 2000 in Brno, Czech Republic, "Eureka" received the judges' award Best Design in the Category of Type. The typeface was later expanded to into a large type system, including "Eureka Sans," and a monospaced variant designed for correspondence and on-screen reading and editing.[8]

Kettler

Lowercase

abcdefghijklmnopqrstuvwxyz

Uppercase

ABCDEFGHIJKLMNOPQRSTUVWXYZ

Punctuation

. , : ; - – — _ ! ? ¡ … • · * + ' " " ' ` ´ ‹ « » ›

Symbols

§ © ® ™ ¶ £ @ & ↓ ↑ → ← ↙ ↗

Ligatures

fi fl

Figures

1234567890

Designer	Eric Olsen

Foundry	Process Type Foundry

Release	2002

World Wide Web	

208 pt	

gA

; " % & (
1 2 4 5 6

Qq Ww Ee Rr Tt

↓ Aa Ss Dd Ff

Yy Xx Cc Vv

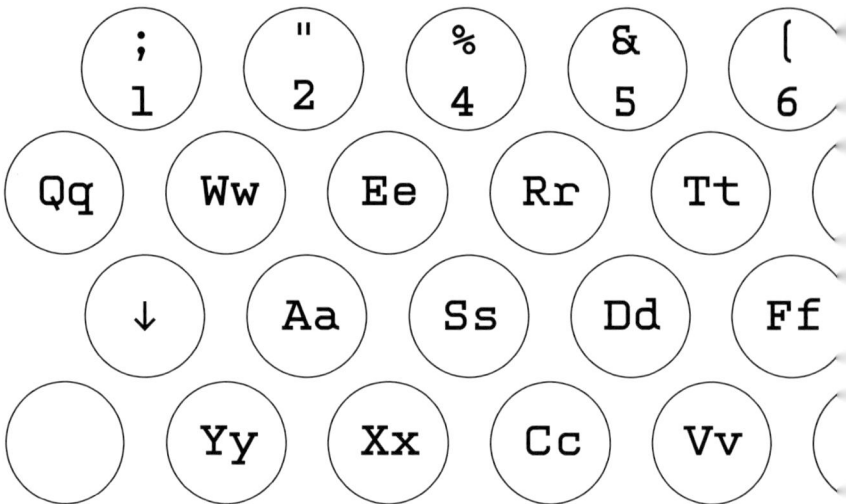

"Kettler" is a simple monospaced font named in tribute
to designer Howard "Bud" Kettler, whose ubiquitous
"Courier" is found on computers everywhere. A subtle
blend of utilitarian slabs serifs and modern curves,
"Kettler" is ideal for tabular information but is also
comfortable in display and headline use.[9]

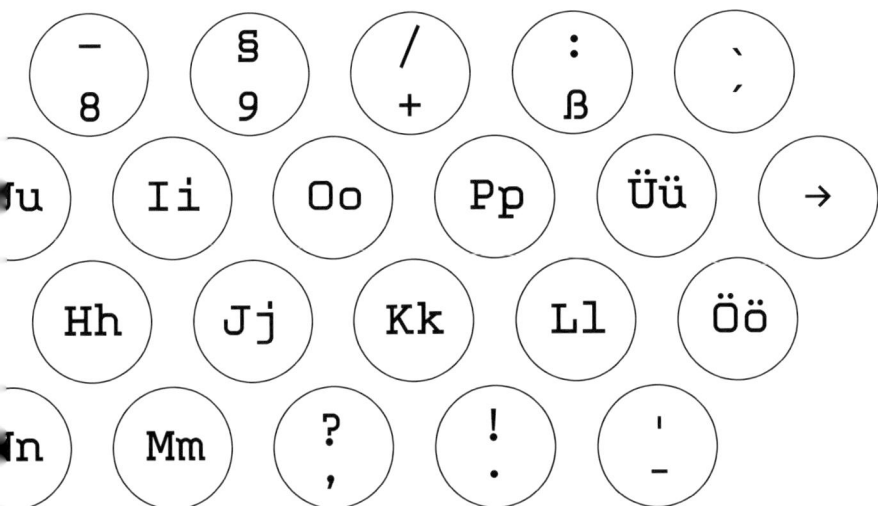

Consolas

Lowercase	abcdefghijklmnopqrstuvwxyz

Uppercase	ABCDEFGHIJKLMNOPQRSTUVWXYZ

Punctuation	.,:;- - — _!?¡…•·*+''""‚›`´‹«»›

Symbols	§©®™¶£€@&

Ligatures	fi fl

Figures	123456789000
	123456789000

Designer	Lucas de Groot

Foundry	LucasFonts

Release	2007

World Wide Web

186 pt

WiS

In 2002, Microsoft invited Luc(as) de Groot to develop a typeface to their planned ClearType Font Collection. Eventually, he would design two: "Consolas" and "Calibri." "Consolas" was the first of the products Luc(as) worked on.

The glyphs across this family of four monospaced fonts all have the same width. Intended for use in programming environments and other circumstances requiring monospaced fonts, "Consolas" has proportions that are closer to normal text. This makes it more reader-friendly than many other monospaced fonts. The look of the text can be tuned to personal taste by varying the number of bars and waves in these letters.

De Groot teamed up with a programmer to test the use of "Consolas" as a font for coding. As the default monospaced font in Windows Vista as well as the Office Suite, "Consolas" became the de facto successor of the ubiquitous "Courier."[10]

Text adapted from the Microsoft brochure
"Now read this." The Microsoft ClearType Font
Collection, edited by John D. Berry (2004).

```
<p>
 coding fonts or not
</p>
```

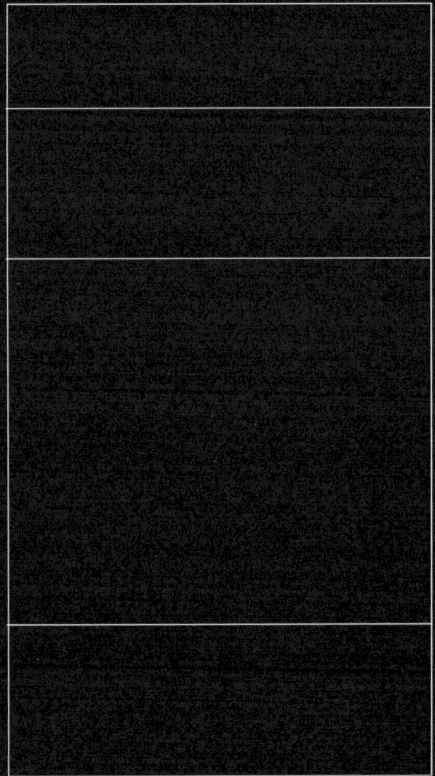

```
<p>
 digital typefaces
</p>
```

```
<p>
 programming
</p>
```

```
<p>
 analog origin
</p>
```

Anonymus Pro

Lowercase	abcdefghijklmnopqrstuvwxyz

Uppercase	ABCDEFGHIJKLMNOPQRSTUVWXYZ

Punctuation	.,:;– – – _!?¡…•·*+"""'' `´‹«»›

Symbols	§©®™¶£€@&Ω⌘↻↵⌐∞▷◆◇✓⇧⬆⌂⬒⊞*⌥⌃

Ligatures	fi fl

Figures	1234567890

Designer	Mark Simonson
Foundry	Mark Simonson Studio
Release	2009
World Wide Web	

186 pt

CsT

"Anonymous Pro" (2009) is a family of four fixed-width fonts designed with coding in mind.[11]

```
#incolde <studio.h>

int main ()
{
printf(''Hello
Anonymus\n'';

return 0,
}
```

Monaco

Lowercase

abcdefghijklmnopqrstuvwxyz

Uppercase

ABCDEFGHIJKLMNOPQRSTUVWXYZ

Punctuation

. , : ; - – — _ ! !! ? ??? !!? ¿ ¡ … ● · * + ' " " ' ‹ « » ›

Symbols

§ © ® ℗ FAX TEL SM TM ¶ £ @ & ◆ ◇ → ↓

Ligatures

fi fl

Figures

1234567890

Designer

Susan Kare, Kris Holmes

Foundry

Apple

Release

2009

156 pt

PgG

"Monaco" is a monospaced sans-serif typeface designed by
Susan Kare and Kris Holmes. The original "Monaco" 9 point
bitmap font was designed so that when a Compact Macintosh
window was displayed full screen, such as for a terminal
emulator program, it would result in a standard text user
interface display of 80 columns by 25 lines.

a	10	Bytes	AAAAAAAAAA
b	20	Bytes	BBBBBBBBBB
c	30	Bytes	CCCCCCCCCC
d	40	Bytes	DDDDDDDDDD
e	50	Bytes	EEEEEEEEEE
f	60	Bytes	FFFFFFFFFF
g	70	Bytes	GGGGGGGGGG
h	80	Bytes	HHHHHHHHHH
i	90	Bytes	IIIIIIIIII

Splendid 66

Lowercase

a b c d e f g h i j k l m n o p q r s t u v w x y z

Uppercase

A B C D E F G H I J K L M N O P Q R S T U V W X Y Z

Punctuation

. , : _ ! ? • + " ' `

Symbols

§ £ &

Figures

1 2 3 4 5 6 7 8 9 0

Designer

Johan Holmdahl

269 pt

C d A

Sudo

Lowercase

abcdefghijklmnopqrstuvwxyz

Uppercase

ABCDEFGHIJKLMNOPQRSTUVWXYZ

Punctuation

.,:;- - – _!?¡…•·*+'""''\'‹‹«»›

Symbols

§©®™¶£€@&℮↑↓⇔⇧⌂⌖⌗⌐⌙⌨Ⅲ▷⠿▦▪□▽●◻◺★⚀⊠⊗

Ξ⊣☺☼♀♂♠♡♥♦♪♫▶⊙⊠‖√☌★✶∷⌗▶↦☆☆⌂▯⊞◁⊏⊠☊☉⊕

Ligatures

fi fl

Figures

12345678900

Designer

Jens Kutílek

Release

2009

World Wide Web

190 pt

ByM

Jens Kutílek

Designer of "Sudo"

There are many reasons why most programmers still prefer monospaced fonts. All letters have the same width in all weights. Proportional alternates are available for some letters via OpenType layout features.

println println println println println println println println println println println pri

When some letter forms are ambiguous in prosa, we can easily read
them because we know the context. But when coding, all characters have
to be unmistakably recognizable. It is common to add serifs to an
uppercase "I" or a hook to the lowercase "l." I don't care very much
for dotted or slashed zeros, so I decided to make all numbers one
line width smaller than the uppercase letters. They still stand out
enough because most code is in lowercase anyway.

This is a first: As far as I know, "Sudo" is the first and only font to
feature what I like to call "coder's quotes." Some programming languages use the acute and grave accents as a replacement for opening
or closing quotes. The standalone accents in "Sudo" are much bigger
than the ones on the accented letters and work well together with the
straight and typo-graphic quotes.[12]

ntln println println println println println println println println println println println println

María Ramos is a type and graphic designer from Santiago de Compostela in Spain. Since 2015 she has made typewriter typefaces to the subject of her research. She deals with the question of a style of typewriters, which features define typewriter typefaces and their historical and contemporary usage. She has given several lectures and published articles such as "Type design for typewriters, Olivetti" or "Typewriter typefaces and their influence on new digital fonts."

Your research about typefaces for typewriters is one of a few — besides there is
much research about the typewriter as an
instrument. What was the reason for you to
start this research? What motivated you?

> The research started while I was at Reading, doing the MA in Typeface Design. All happened in an academic environment, where I had the support of my supervisor and I benefited from the network and materials provided by the university. My reasons for choosing this particular topic are quite random, there is of course a personal interest but I had never thought of this before. There was a moment at the beginning of the course when we had to define the topic for our dissertations. I knew it had to be something I would enjoy researching because I was going to spend much time on this. I had a short list of possible topics and I finally picked this one for two main reasons, it seemed to be a lack of information and I felt a personal connection to it. I did experienced and learned to use the typewriter myself when I was a child.

Monospaced typefaces were born with mechanical
typewriters. The first fast writing, the
typing, and the mechanization of handwriting
were initially more revolutionary than
typefaces with fixed spaced letters. The
introduction of the computer and new software
programs have changed type design and the
usage of monospaced typefaces. A great number
of digital typefaces are monospaced or have
a mono or semi-mono weight. Typewriter typefaces did not disappear. Why do they — in
your opinion — still exist? Why are they so
fascinating for many?

> I think we have barely scratched the surface in monospace type design. It is great to look at the past and learn from what others have done before but we need to take our designs further. I would like to see more inventiveness in monospace fonts. I think type designers need to free themselves from conventional typewriter features. It is true though that the variety in monospaced type design is getting better. We have discovered new typewriter references in the last decade, for instance, it is not hard no to find script of italic monospaced typefaces today. We shouldn't limit our designs to conventional references. There were so many beautiful designs created for typewriters! It's still an incredible source for inspiration.

How has the design of typewriter typefaces
changed? What is worth noting? Can you give a
short insight in the evolution of monospaced
typeface design?

María Ramos   72

I'd like to separate these two terms first, monospaced type-faces and typewriter typefaces in digital means are two different things to me. If we talk about digital typewriter typefaces I'd say there is something unique about the original source. Monospaced typefaces, as you've said, were born from mechanical constraints. The problems caused by the machine became an opportunity for type designers, who were able to depart from conventions in printing type, using new proportions, and some new features.

Besides their peculiarities in shape, the irregular contours and the uneven color in text was also part of their charm. What do designers find so fascinating in these old designs? The answer is clear to me, they were inventive and, contrary to what one might expect, constraints make it possible to have a certain amount of freedom in type design.

The design of monospaced typefaces was set by the technical limitations of the type-writer. The strict positioning of each sign and the resulting restrictions, or certain "basic principles" define at the same time the aesthetics. Can you tell a little bit about the influence on typewriter typefaces on monospaced typefaces now?

The origin is clear, the history of monospaced typefaces started with typewriters and they will always be connected in some way. Many of the things we can see today in digital monospaced fonts have their roots in typewriter type design. Think for example in how we solve the darkness in a mono-space serif "m" or how we fill the gap in the "J." I think, in essence, digital monospaced fonts will always be linked to the typewriter, which doesn't mean they can't depart in shape from their references.

What do you think about the future of mono-spaced typefaces? How will they evolve?

I am really not good with predictions so I'll just say I'd like to be surprised by what type designers have to offer.

Short question in the end: What is you favorite monospaced font? Do you have one?

This is a short and hard question, choosing only one is almost impossible. I am gonna mention three instead, three examples that I like in different styles, *Tabulamore Script, Input,* and *Operator.*

Find out more about María Ramos' work and her research on marsidesino.com

Aperçu Mono

Lowercase	abcdefghijklmnopqrstuvwxyz

Uppercase	ABCDEFGHIJKLMNOPQRSTUVWXYZ

Punctuation	. , : ; - – — _ ! ? ¡ … • · * + ` " „ " ' ` ´ ‹ « » ›

Symbols	§©®™¶£€@&

Ligatures	fi fl

Figures	1234567890

Designer	The Entente
Foundry	Colophon Foundry
Release	2010
World Wide Web	

170 pt

SmR

"Aperçu" was launched in December 2009, and was trialled and tested throughout a number of design commissions. The conceit behind Aperçu was to create a synopsis or amalgamation of classic realist typefaces: "Johnston," "Gill Sans," "Neuzeit,"and "Franklin Gothic."

"Aperçu" is available in both a proportional family of eight weights – Thin, ExtraLight, Light, Regular, Medium, Bold, ExtraBold, and Black – with corresponding italics, as well as a Monospaced type family of four weights – Light, Regular, Medium, and Bold.[13]

A a   B b   C c

D d   E e   F f

G g   H h   I i

J j   K k   L l

M m   ? !   N n

O o   P p   Q q

R r   S s   T t

U u   V v   W w

X x   Y y   Z z

Calico Mono Ink Trapped

Lowercase

abcdefghijklmnopqrstuvwxyz

Uppercase

ABCDEFGHIJKLMNOPQRSTUVWXYZ

Punctuation

. , : ; - – — _ ! ? ¡ … · · * + ' " " ' ` ´ ‹ « » ›

Symbols

§ © ® ™ ¶ | £ € @ & ◊ ♥

Figures

1234567890

Designer	Mirage Design Studio

Release	2010

World Wide Web	

176 pt

FsK

R

AU

typing
writing
hiking
reading
sharing
caring
wearing

M

Maison Mono

Lowercase

abcdefghijklmnopqrstuvwxyz

Uppercase

ABCDEFGHIJKLMNOPQRSTUVWXYZ

Punctuation

. , : ; - – — _ ! ? ¡ … • · * + ' " " ' ` ´ ‹ « » ›

Symbols

§ © ℗ ® ™ ¶ £ € @ &

Figures

1234567890

Designer	Timo Gaessner
Foundry	Milieu Grotesque
Release	2010
World Wide Web	

169 pt

GtH

1 2

3 4 5

6 7 8

9 0

"Maison" is a mono-lined grotesque constructed using rigid elements to achieve a minimalist industrial feel in homage to the early twentieth century modernist design concepts. Originally created as a monospaced typeface family — with less optical corrections than its successor "Maison Neue" — "Maison" has been further developed to work equally in both monospaced and proportional alignments.[14]

Ubuntu Mono

Lowercase

abcdefghijklmnopqrstuvwxyz

Uppercase

ABCDEFGHIJKLMNOPQRSTUVWXYZ

Punctuation

. , : ; - – — _ ! ? ¡ … • · * + ' " " ' ` ´ ‹ « » ›

Symbols

§©®™¶£€@&□□⁰⁸@◊▨▨▊

Ligatures

fi fl

Figures

1234567890

Designer	Dalton Maag
Foundry	Google Fonts
Release	2010–2011
World Wide Web	

192 pt

UmY

Suisse Int'l Mono

Lowercase

abcdefghijklmnopqrstuvwxyz

Uppercase

ABCDEFGHIJKLMNOPQRSTUVWXYZ

Punctuation

. , : ; - – — _ ! ? ¡ … • · * + ' " " ' ` ´ ‹ « » ›

Symbols

§©®™¶£€@&◊

Ligatures

Figures

1234567890

Designer	Ian Party, Swiss Typefaces
Foundry	Swiss Typefaces
Release	2011
World Wide Web	

About

Suisse Int'l Mono is the monospaced variant of *Suisse Int'l.* All characters have the same width, like on a typewriter. *Suisse Int'l Mono* comes in handy when you want to fuse the objectivity of a Swiss Grotesk with the credibility of a typewritten document.[16]

163 pt

ZaK

Atlas Typewriter

Lowercase	abcdefghijklmnopqrstuvwxyz

Uppercase	ABCDEFGHIJKLMNOPQRSTUVWXYZ

Punctuation	., :; - - — _ ! ? ¡ … • · * + ' " " ' ` ´ ‹ « » ›

Symbols	§©℗®™¶£€@&

Ligatures	fi fl

Figures	12345678900

Designer	Susana Carvalho, Kai Bernau, Ilya Ruderman
Foundry	Commercial Type
Release	2012
World Wide Web	

155 pt

AfQ

"Atlas Typewriter" is a distinctive monospaced sans, well suited for a wide range of uses, from art catalogs to personal correspondence, through to data visualization. Rather than hewing closely to the model of existing mono-spaced typefaces, "Atlas Typewriter" aims for an even, readable texture with the same clean and effortless tone as the Grotesk. Characters like "f" and "t" are distinc-tively symmetrical, while the "r" is unadorned with extraneous serifs or terminals, making it eater and less distracting in text than in a typical monospaced sans.[17]

10

mit
Fin

gern

Blue Mono

Lowercase

abcdefghijkLmnopqrstuvwxyz

Uppercase

ABCDEFGHIJKLMNOPQRSTUVWXYZ

Punctuation

. , : ; - – — _ ! ? ¡ … · · * + ' " " ' ` ´ ‹ « » ›

Symbols

§©®™¶£€@&&Ω▶▣▲▼ ◄ ► ▲ ▼ ←→ ↘ ↗ ↗ ↖ ↑ ↓ ►

Figures

1234567890

1234567890

Designer	Jérémie Nuel

Foundry	VolcanoType

Release	2012

World Wide Web	

184 pt

OLF

tippen

klakkern

kling

nachschieben

vertippt

Löschband

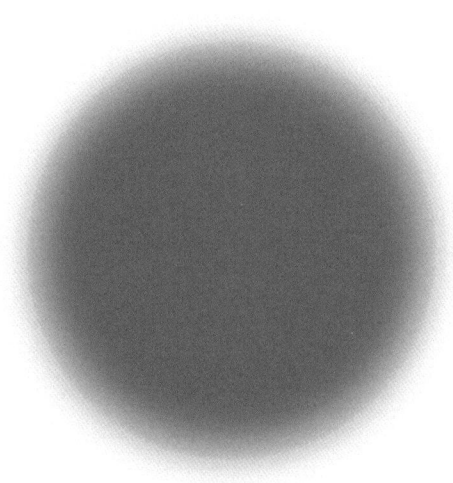

As a binary system, at the junction to two antagonist drawings, the "Blue (Not) Mono" typeface is an hybrid between the monospace and the humanistic sans-serif families.[18]

Pitch

Lowercase

abcdefghijklmnopqrstuvwxyz

Uppercase

ABCDEFGHIJKLMNOPQRSTUVWXYZ

Punctuation

. , : ; - – — _ ! ? ¡ … • · * + ' " " ' ` ' ‹ « » ›

Symbols

§ © ® ™ ♪ £ € @ & Ω → ♠ ♡ ◇ ♣ ♤ ♥ ♦ ♧ ℗ ←

Figures

1234567890

1 2 3 4 5 6 7 8 9 0

Designer	Kris Sowersby
Foundry	Klim Type Foundry
Release	2012
World Wide Web	

209 pt

AgH

Pitch is a love letter by Kris Sowersby to the typewriter

A typewriter has a singular purpose putting letters onto a page. Put the paper in, stab away at the keys and letters instantly appear. It is tactile, analog, immediate. The German "Schreibmaschine" means typewriter, and upon closer inspection is literally composed of the words writing machine. For me this is the perfect definition for a typewriter.

With a legacy of functionality, romance and literary seriousness, writers and journalists used typewriters to great effect. No formatting, no typographic styling just the writer and their words. Its a humble, beautiful object, a representation of mechanical refinement, and industrial design. It is an honest machine, it does exactly what you tell it.

The honest aesthetic of the typewritten text these writing machines produce is wonderful. I wanted to capture this particular aesthetic with "Pitch." The aesthetics of typewritten text are largely due to three things monospacing, type style, and the artefacts of struck paper.[19]

<u>a love letter to the typewriter</u>

writing machine writing machine writing machine
writing machine writing machine writing machine

Schreibmaschine Schreibmaschine Schreibmaschine
Schreibmaschine Schreibmaschine Schreibmaschine

writing machine writing machine writing machine
writing machine writing machine writing machine

Schreibmaschine Schreibmaschine Schreibmaschine
Schreibmaschine Schreibmaschine Schreibmaschine

writing machine writing machine writing machine
writing machine writing machine writing machine

Schreibmaschine Schreibmaschine Schreibmaschine
Schreibmaschine Schreibmaschine Schreibmaschine

writing machine writing machine writing machine
writing machine writing machine writing machine

Schreibmaschine Schreibmaschine Schreibmaschine
Schreibmaschine Schreibmaschine Schreibmaschine

writing machine writing machine writing machine
writing machine writing machine writing machine

Schreibmaschine Schreibmaschine Schreibmaschine
Schreibmaschine Schreibmaschine Schreibmaschine

Roboto Mono

Lowercase

abcdefghijklmnopqrstuvwxyz

Uppercase

ABCDEFGHIJKLMNOPQRSTUVWXYZ

Punctuation

.,.;- – — _!¡!?¡…•·*+'""''`´‹«»›

Symbols

§©®™¶£€@&◊

Figures

1234567890

Designer	Christian Robertson
Foundry	Google Fonts
Release	2012
World Wide Web	

About — Roboto Mono is a monospaced addition to the Roboto type family. Like the other members of the Roboto family, the fonts are optimized for readability on screens across a wide variety of devices and reading environments. While the monospaced version is related to its variable width cousin, it doesn't hesitate to change forms to better fit the constraints of a monospaced environment.[20]

167 pt

UiX

Source Code Pro

Lowercase

abcdefghijklmnopqrstuvwxyz

Uppercase

ABCDEFGHIJKLMNOPQRSTUVWXYZ

Punctuation

. , : ; - – — _ ! ? ¡ … • · * + ' " " ' ` ´ ‹ « » ›

Symbols

§ © ® ™ ℠ ℮ ¶ | £ € ₽ ₦ ₱ ₲ ₵ ₹ ₺ @ & ℗ ☐ ☑ ♪ √ ← ↑ → ↓

Ligatures

fi fl

Figures

1234567890

1234567890

Designer	Paul D. Hunt

Foundry	Adobe

Release	2012

World Wide Web

About

Source Code was designed by Paul D. Hunt as a companion to Source Sans. This complementary family was adapted from the Source design due to a request to create a monospaced version for coding applications. Source Code preserves the design features and vertical proportions of Source Sans, but alters the glyph widths so that they are uniform across all glyphs and weights.[21]

180 pt

XgC

GT Pressura Mono

Lowercase	abcdefghijklmnopqrstuvwxyz

Uppercase	ABCDEFGHIJKLMNOPQRSTUVWXYZ

Punctuation	. , : ; - – — _ ! ? ¡ … • • * + ' " " ' ` ´ ‹ « » ›

Symbols	§©®™¶£€@&Ω→₩₮₴₹₺₽฿₡№∂ø∆∏∑½←

Ligatures	fi fl

Figures	1234567890

Designer	Marc Kappeler, Dominik Huber

Foundry	Grilli Type

Release	2012–2017

World Wide Web

170 pt

ZqR

"GT Pressura" is inspired by metal type printing history as well as engineered letters stamped onto shipping boxes. It uses the visual gesture of ink spreading under pressure as a stylistic device, offering an alternative to more spindly typefaces of the digital age.[22]

8 pt	shipping boxes filled with printing history
9 pt	shipping boxes filled with printing history
10 pt	shipping boxes filled with printing history
11 pt	shipping boxes filled with printing history
12 pt	shipping boxes filled with printing histo
14 pt	shipping boxes filled with printing
18 pt	shipping boxes filled with
24 pt	shipping boxes filled
30pt	shipping boxes f.
36 pt	shipping boxes
48 pt	shipping b
60 pt	shipping
72 pt	shippin

Input Mono

Lowercase

abcdefghijklmnopqrstuvwxyz

Uppercase

ABCDEFGHIJKLMNOPQRSTUVWXYZ

Punctuation

., :;- - — _!?¡…••*+′″‴‵\`´ ‹«»›

Symbols

§©®™¶£€℮@&*←↓↕↔↨↓■□■▫▸●○♀♂♀♂♠♣♥♦♪

⚡🔒⏰☇▶◀🐞

Ligatures

ij

Figures

123456789000

Designer	David Jonathan Ross
Foundry	DJR
Release	2016
World Wide Web	

About Part of the *Input* series. Originally issued by Font Bureau. Moved to DJR in 2016. *Input Mono* comes in 56 styles; 4 widths in 7 weights each, plus italics.

163 pt

EiP

Usually, monospaced fonts aren't great for setting normal
text, but they have become the de facto standard for setting code. Since all characters are constrained to the same
fixed width, the page becomes a grid of characters, something that drastically simplified the mechanics of typesetting in early computers. However, monospacing comes at
an aesthetic cost: wide characters are forced to squeeze;
narrow characters are forced to stretch. Uppercase letters
look skinny next to lowercase, and bold characters don't
have enough room to get very bold.

PID	COMMAND	%CPU	TIME	#TH	#WQ	#PORT
25645	top	16.3	00:02.03	1/1	0	22
25642	bash	0.0	00:00.01	1	0	19
25641	login	0.0	00:00.02	2	0	30
25634	mdworker	0.0	00:00.07	3	0	56
25624	mdworker	0.0	00:00.14	4	0	58
25591	mdworker	0.0	00:00.14	3	0	56
25571	com.apple.iC	0.0	00:00.31	5	0	87
25414	installd	0.0	00:00.52	2	0	49
25366	com.apple.We	0.0	00:00.07	4	1	135

As writing and managing code becomes more complex, today's sophisticated coding environments are evolving to include everything from breakpoint markers to code folding and syntax highlighting. The typography of code should evolve as well, to explore possibilities beyond one font style, one size, and one character width.[23]

David Jonathan Ross

#MREGS	MEN	RPRVT	PRUG	CMPRS	VPRVT	VSIZE
50	7536K	7312K	0B	0B	74M	2443M
32	656k	488k	0B	0B	28M	2395M
52	1056K	7732K	0B	0B	88M	2446M
70	2836K	1864K+	0B	0B	53M+	2446M
92	4112K	3008K	0B	0B	91M	2484M
105	3704K	2440K	0B	0B	81M	2474M
86	3664K	2884K	0B	0B	98M	2480M
192	18M	177M	0B	5876B	120M	2501M
120	1312K	812K	0B	3680B	92M	3524M

Airport Mono

Lowercase

abcdefghijklmnopqrstuvwxyz

Uppercase

ABCDEFGHIJKLMNOPQRSTUVWXYZ

Punctuation

. , : ; - – — _ ! ? ¿ ¡ … · · * + ' " " ' ' ‹ « » ›

Symbols

§ © ® ℗ ™ ¶ £ € ₴ & ◊ □ ○ ★ ☆ ✦ ← ↑ → ↓ ↖ ↗ ↘ ↙

Ligatures

IJ ij

Figures

1234567890

Designer	Piero Di Biase
Foundry	Think Work Observe
Release	2014-2017
World Wide Web	

165 pt

QsT

Time	Flight		Destination	Gate
15:15	2547	→	MILAN	20A
15:15	4875	→	LUXEMBOURG	18B
15:20	8571	→	PRAGUE	5E
15:25	5721	→	GOTHENBURG	7D
15:40	6785	→	VIENNA	M5
15:45	2002	→	BRUSSELS	2C
16:10	5478	→	REYKJAVIK	15F
16:20	5420	→	AMSTERDAM	5D
16:25	2630	→	MUNICH	13B
16:30	8564	→	LISBON	17C
16:40	1399	→	WARSAW	7C
16:40	7608	→	ZAGREB	18A
17:16	6592	→	PARIS	4E
17:32	1394	→	MOSCOW	17A
17:58	1552	→	PORTO	3B

Departure

"Airport Mono" is a monospaced sans-serif typeface
inspired by military airports signage. Available
in Regular, Medium, and Bold.[24]

SXF

CINDIE D

Uppercase

Uppercase

ABCDEFGHIJKLM
NOPQRSTUVWXYZ

Punctuation

. , ... : ; ! ¡ " " ' ' ... – – – __ ?
¡ ... ■ · * + ' " " , ` ´ ‹ « » ›

Symbols

§ © ® ™ ¶ € £ $ ¢ @ & % ∗ ∞ ◊

Figures

1234567890

Designer	LEWIS MCCUFFIE
Foundry	LEWIS MCCUFFIE TYPE
Release	2016
World Wide Web	

119 pt

MJ

A B C
D E F G
H I J K
L M N O
P Q R S
T U V W
X Y Z

"CINDIE" IS A MONOSPACED TYPEFACE
WITH FOUR SUPERIMPOSED WIDTHS
INSPIRED BY OPTOMETRIC FONTS AND
MAGAZINE GRIDS. SOFTENED CORNERS
AND MIXED COUNTERS ADD TO CINDIE'S
READABILITY.[25]

Monoela

| Lowercase | abcdefghijklmnopqrstuvwxyz |

| Uppercase | ABCDEFGHIJKLMNOPQRSTUVWXYZ |

| Punctuation | .,:;- – — _!?¡…•·*+'""''`´‹«»› |

| Symbols | §©®™¶£€@& |

| Ligatures | f fi fl ʦ ij IJ |

| Figures | 1234567890 |

Designer	André Leonhardt, Dennis Michaelis

Foundry	Interfont

Release	2016

World Wide Web

185 pt

SeP

Inspired by the mechanical typewriter, *Monoela* interprets its characteristics in a contemporary way. Objective and rational at first sight, *Monoela's* character becomes visible in striking shapes and unexpected proportions. Designed by André Leonhardt and Dennis Michaelis, who together as "Interfont" design typefaces with strong formal and conceptual demands.

Why did you decide to design a monospaced
typeface? And what is the appeal of non-
proportional typefaces to you?

> We saw the limitation of filling a fixed tracking distance with complex and less complex shapes as an exciting challenge that we wanted to face.

How did the idea for "Monoela" come about?
What stands behind it?

> Dennis was a typewriter fan even before he started his bachelor's degree in 2008. He experimented a lot with the instrument. During his internship at the Stan Hema agency, he met Leo. We both shared our interest in typefaces and typeface design.

> At some point the idea came up to develop our own monospace typeface in order to return the letters to an analog typewriter with the help of a 3D printer — from analog to digital to analog. Ultimately, a digital font with five styles was created. However, the idea of a *Monoela* typewriter has remained just an idea.

To what extent has the instrument of the
typewriter influenced you?

> We found it exciting to put the historical effect of the letter forms of old typewriters into a contemporary context. So at *Monoela* we tried to build a bridge between old and new.

Can you give an insight into the development
process of "Moneola?" Do you prefer analog or
digital methods when developing fonts?

> Dennis first outlines his ideas with a pen on paper before sitting down at the computer. Leo, on the other hand, designs and rejects his ideas directly in FontLab or sketches them on a tablet.

Above all, "Monoela" owns a good legibility.
Was that a obstacle in the conception?
How do you rate the legibility of
monospaced typefaces?

> We are pleased that you find *Monoela* legible, that was not our intention. Our idea was to develop a typeface for designing. Many non-proportional typefaces are balanced and harmonious in themselves, but they are not suitable for contemporary media design. We have deliberately designed independent and sometimes also unique glyphs that makes the typeface striking and creates an exciting font. Readability was never a priority.

Schreiben? Tippen!

Schreiben? Tippen!

Schreiben? Tippen!

Schreiben? Tippen!

Schreiben? Tippen!

How do you see the trend in the design and
type design world to use monospaced typefaces again? Or do you think it exists?

> We rather see a trend towards strange, striking typefaces
> away from a total harmonization of shapes and spacing.
> Monospace fonts may fit in there.

When do you like to use a monospaced font?

> That depends from project to project and the overall design.
> There is no overall or mandatory requirement for this.

And a short question at the very end:
Do you have another favorite monospaced
font besides "Monoela?"

> Definitely: *Maison Mono* and *IBM Plex Mono.*

Find out more about André Leonhardt
and Dennis Michaelis on interfont.net

Space Mono

Lowercase

abcdefghijklmnopqrstuvwxyz

Uppercase

ABCDEFGHIJKLMNOPQRSTUVWXYZ

Punctuation

. , : ; - – — _ ! ? ¡ … • · ＊ + ' " " ' ´ ‹ « » ›

Ligatures

Ú Ú

Figures

1234567890

1234567890

Designer	Colophon Foundry
Foundry	Google Fonts
Release	2016
World Wide Web	

170 pt

WyD

"Space Mono" — whose name inverts its own typographic classifica- tion — is a monospace (sometimes called fixed-width, fixed-pitch, or non-proportional) typeface that comprises Regular, Italic, Bold, and Bold Italic cuts, commis- sioned for the 2016 update of Google Fonts.

While certain type classifications (Grotesque, Humanist, etc.) describe historical context or appearance, a monospace type doesn't describe its character, but rather its construction. And while that construction often dictates form (an "m" may get smushed into its container; an "i" extended outwards with foot and bar), we found it interest- ing that despite these formal constraints, monospaced type is widely used in editorial settings to give a certain style or feel rather than hit a specific char- acter count or meet a technical limitation.

Delving into this process got us thinking about what monospace means to us: If we drew a na- tively monospaced typeface as an homage to our abstract percep- tions of that typographic desig- nation, what form would it take? Maybe instead of trying to opti- mize for readability or perfor- mance, or capture an amalgamation of monospace attributes, we could instead mine our cultural asso- ciations and exploit the limita- tions of fixed-width type.

P

M

So while the click-clack of the
typewriter occurred to us for
a brief moment (Film Noir!
Olivetti! Sottsass!), the ideal-
ized monospace that is closer
to our hearts and more aligned
with our cultural touchstones
are the displays, monitors, and
screens of Speculative Fiction —
the imagined or not-yet-real
interfaces of canonical Sci-Fi
films and television programs.

Most monospaced types are dictated by text-intensive usage at
small point sizes, but we were
captivated by the possibility of
a monospace writ large, as it
is in our collective mind's eye:
a few words projected on a large
display, rendered in simplified,
appealingly vague pieces of
warning or counsel that only a
trained operator understands,
all witnessed via screen-within-
imaginary-screen, aboard inter-
planetary vessels and hovering
automobiles.[26]

Colophon Foundry

Droulers

Lowercase

abodefghijklmnopqrstuvwxyz

Uppercase

ABCDEFGHIJKLMNOPQRSTUVWXYZ

Punctuation

. , : ; - – — _ ! ? ¡ … • · * + ' ' " " ' ` ‹ « » ›

Symbols

§©®™¶℥€@℈◇□□□□□□●❒¶Ω❒⌧⎙∧∨⇗∖⌐◖
◆⌦☺☹☑♠♥♧⌂⚠✂✁◈☀✿⚘

Ligatures

fi fl fj fb fh fk ft ff ffj ffl ffb ffh ffk fft

Figures

1234567890

Designer	Julia Joffre, Yoann Minet,
	Camille Prandi

Foundry	Bureau Brut

Release	2017

World Wide Web	

170 pt

GhF

"Droulers" was designed for a book spanning the life and work of the dancer and choreographer Pierre Droulers. The typeface draws upon printed matter found in "Droulers'" personal archive and in particular some typewritten notes. Exploring both the specific rhythm and shapes of typewriter alphabets, the design is inspired by the distortions and accidents generated by this technology: letters obstructed by ink, closing counter forms, and soon. "Droulers'" true strength appears in text setting at small sizes, but at a larger scale each letter gets its primitive graphic power back.[27]

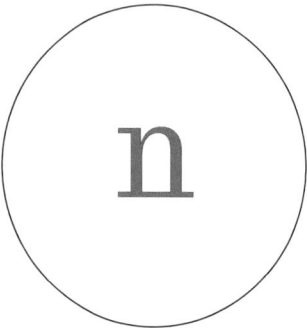

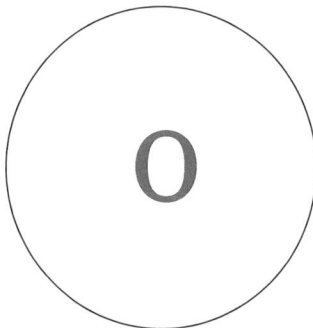

n o

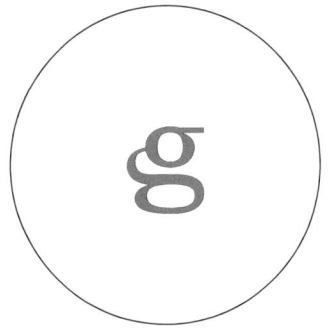

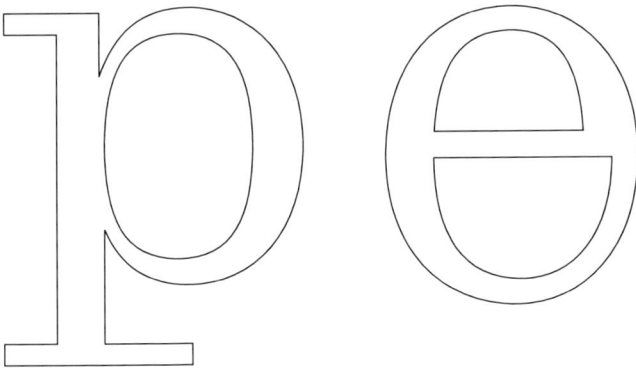

IBM Plex Mono

Lowercase

abcdefghijklmnopqrstuvwxyz

Uppercase

ABCDEFGHIJKLMNOPQRSTUVWXYZ

Punctuation

. , : ; - – — _ ! ? ¡ … • · * + ' " " ' ` ' ‹ « » ›

Symbols

§©®™¶£@&¢€₦₨₩₪₫€₭₮₱₲₴₵₡↑↓↔↕◊

Ligatures

fi fl

Figures

123456789000

Designer	Mike Abbink, Paul van der Laan, Pieter van Rosmalen
Foundry	IBM, Bold Monday
Release	2017
World Wide Web	

170 pt

NfG

Mankind and Machine

When we set out to create a typeface that was unmistakably IBM, our own history was our greatest source of inspiration. IBM has always served as a medium between mankind and machine. Between the natural and the engineered. The emotional and rational. The classic and the cutting-edge. Our most important job is to help humanity and technology move forward together. "IBM Plex" brings these relationships to life through letter forms.[28]

The Right Choice

We needed "Plex" to be a distinctive, yet timeless workhorse — an alternative to "Helvetica Neue" for this new era. The Grotesque style was the perfect fit. Not only do these typefaces balance human and rational elements, the Grotesque style also came about during the Industrial Age (when IBM was born).[29]

Mike Abbink, Paul van der Laan, Pieter van Rosmalen

Selectric "golf ball." Long before uploading fonts into a type manager, IBM printed physical catalogs for Selectric's interchangeable type "golf balls."

LTC Remington Typewriter

Lowercase

abcdefghijklmnopqrstuvwxyz

Uppercase

ABCDEFGHIJKLMNOPQRSTUVWXYZ

Punctuation

. , : ; - – — _ ! !! ? ‽ ¿ ¡ ... • · * + ' " " ' ` ´ ‹ « » ›

Symbols

§ © ® ™ ¶ £ € @ & ◇ ☺ ☻ ▫ ⊡ ⊞ ⊠ ⊟ □ ◻ ✿ ✝

Ligatures

fi fl

Figures

1234567890

①②③④⑤⑥⑦⑧⑨⑩

Designer	Frederic Goudy, Paul D. Hunt, Lanston Type Company
Foundry	P22
Release	2018
World Wide Web	

169 pt

JtS

The original designer
of Remington Typewriter
is unknown. It was one
of the earliest Lanston
Monotype designs. The
Italic was designed by
Frederic Goudy in 1927.
His approach was to
make an unconventional
typewriter form that
looked well spaced even
though all letters
shared the same width.[30]

Monument Grotesk Mono

Lowercase

abcdefghijklmnopqrstuvwxyz

Uppercase

ABCDEFGHIJKLMNOPQRSTUVWXYZ

Punctuation

. , : ; - – — _ ! ? ¿ ¡ … • · * + ' " " ' ` ´ ‹ « » › ↑ ↓ ↖ ↘

Symbols

§ © ® ™ ¶ £ € @ & ◇ ☮ ☯ ☯ ▫ ❑ ❒ ❐ ❏ ❒ ◻ ◻ ✡ ✚

Ligatures

fi fl

Figures

12345678900

①②③④⑤⑥⑦⑧⑨⓪

Designer	Larissa Kasper, Rosario Florio, Robert Janes, Fabiola Mejía

Foundry	Dinamo

Release	2018

World Wide Web	

About	*Monument Grotesk* owes its point de départ to a few contours Kasper-Florio stumbled upon online in 2013 in Palmer and Rey's *New Specimen Book,* 1884, on page 81. The find relied on a sturdy and compact skeleton, high vertical contrast, and surprisingly sharp end strokes.[31]

169 pt

FmR

Simon Mono Light

Lowercase

abcdefghijklmnopqrstuvwxyz

Uppercase

ABCDEFGHIJKLMNOPQRSTUVWXYZ

Punctuation

. , : ; - – — _ ! ? ¡ … · • * + ' " " ' ` ´ ‹ « » ›

Symbols

©™£@&

Ligatures

fi fl www

Figures

1234567890

Digitizer	JP Haynie, Robert Janes
Foundry	Dinamo
Release	2018
World Wide Web	

175 pt

LaJ

"Simon" is a modern typewriter typeface, sporting sharp terminals and large punctuation. ITC American Typewriter was the main source of research, however Simon's proportions and forms are drawn for contemporary usage: unnecessary details such as ball terminals and flaring serifs were removed in favor of a more industrial drawing style.

type  write

mono 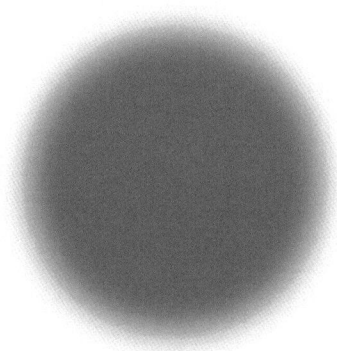 face

In 2019–2020 "Simon" was extended to a full family of weights. It was first used as the main text typeface in "Shoplifters 8: New Type Design by Actual Source." [32]

Plastic

Lowercase

abcdefghijkℓlmnopqrstuvwxyz

abcdefghijkℓlmnopqrstuvwxyz

Uppercase

ABCDEFGHIJKLMNOPQRSTUVWXYZ

ABCDEFGHIJKLMNOPQRSTUVWXYZ

ABCDEFGHIJKLM
NOPQRSTUVWXYZ

ABCDEFGHIJKLM
NOPQRSTUVWXYZ

Punctuation

. , : ; - - - _ ▽ ? ? ȧ .. • · * + ' " " ' ` ´ ♡ ☆ △ ○

. , : ; - - - _ ▽ ? ? ȧ .. • · * + ' " " ' ` ´ ♡ ☆ △ ○

Symbols

§©®™¶£(§)&

§©®™¶£(§)&

Ligatures

ff fi fl

ff fi fl

Figures

1234567890 1234567890

1234567890 1234567890

Designer

Jitka Janečková, Ivana Paľečková

Release

2018

World Wide Web

154 pt

XgS

"Plastic" is a monospace variable font
based on four masters – Chain Black,
Chain Thin, Simple Black, and Simple
Thin. The variable format enables live
interpolation between four extremes
on two axes: the stroke weight and character openness. "Plastic" is inspired
by the Czechoslovak socialist phenomenon of the 80s – a plastic toy "Céčka."
The chaining feature of the toy was the
ground principle for the concept. This
feature graduates in the Chain Styles.
The conventional construction of the
Simple styles broadens the use of the
typeface. Font offers a stylistic set
of expanded capitals and numbers which
makes the headline setting even more
extravagant.

The first design of the font was created as a student project at the Academy
of Fine Arts and Design in Bratislava,
under the guidance of Palo Bálik and
Michal Tornyai.[33]

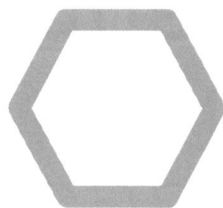

Jitka Janečková, Ivana Palečková

plastic simple
plastic simple
plastic simple
plastic simple
plastic simple
plastic simple
plastic chain
plastic chain
plastic chain
plastic chain
plastic chain
plastic chain

The Future Mono

Lowercase

abcdefghijklmnopqrstuvwxyz

Uppercase

ABCDEFGHIJKLMNOPQRSTUVWXYZ

Punctuation

. , : ; - – — _ ! ? ¡ … • · * + ' // // ' ` ´

Symbols

§©®™¶£₫&™

Figures

1234567890

Designer	Kris Sowersby, Noe Blanco

Foundry	Klim Type Foundry, Future Fonts

Release	2018

World Wide Web	

158 pt

M+H

Imagine if Paul Renner moved to Japan and Kyota Sugimoto asked him to adapt Futura to a typewriter.[34]

Basier Mono

Lowercase	abcdefghijklmnopqrstuvwxyz

Uppercase	ABCDEFGHIJKLMNOPQRSTUVWXYZ

Punctuation	. , : ; - – — _ ! ? ¡ … • · * + ' " " ' ` ´ ‹ « » ›

Symbols	§©®™¶£@&

Figures	1234567890

Designer	Atipo Foundry
Foundry	Atipo Foundry
Release	2019
World Wide Web	

170 pt

U1R

The font for letter lovers and love letters.

"Basier Mono" is based on the "Basier" font
family. Inspired by the International Style,
is a neo-grotesque sans-serif typeface available
in two variants, Circle and Square. The result
is a modern and neutral font family.[35]

Cygnito Mono

Lowercase

abcdefghijklmnopqrstuvwxyz

Uppercase

ABCDEFGHIJKLMNOPQRSTUVWXYZ

Punctuation

.,:;- – — _!?¡…▪·*+''""''`´ ‹«»›

Symbols

§©®™¶£@&←→↑↓↔↕↖↘↙↗↺↻↲−≅≈≠≡≤≥

Figures

1234567890

Designer	Radinal Riki
Foundry	ATK Studio
Release	2019
World Wide Web	

170 pt

XVE

a	10	Bytes	AAAAAAAAAA
b	20	Bytes	BBBBBBBBBB
c	30	Bytes	CCCCCCCCCC
d	40	Bytes	DDDDDDDDDD
e	50	Bytes	EEEEEEEEEE
f	60	Bytes	FFFFFFFFFF
g	70	Bytes	GGGGGGGGGG
h	80	Bytes	HHHHHHHHHH
i	90	Bytes	IIIIIIIIII

Inspired by modernism and industrial graphic design. This is a solid industrial monospaced font with octagon angles (±45°) and octagon structure. Determine the grid and create a complete set of cohesive characters (A-Z) and multi-language characters (Latin based) in either lowercase or uppercase, with consideration for scale, proportion, and balance between the letterform.[36]

Sneak Mono

Lowercase

abcdefghijklmnopqrstuvwxyz

Uppercase

ABCDEFGHIJKLMNOPQRSTUVWXYZ

Punctuation

. , : ; - – — _ ! ? ¡ … · · * + ' " " ' ' ` ´ ‹ « › ›

Symbols

§©®™¶£@&☺◇●⊢↦√

①②③④⑤⑥⑦⑧⑨⑩⓪❶❷❸❹❺❻❼❽❾❿

Figures

1234567890

Designer	Fabian Fohrer

Foundry	TIGHTYPE

Release	**2019**

World Wide Web

About

Sneak is a neo-grotesque typeface, featuring several reversed characters, such as its distinctive "S." *Sneak* is available in five weights with corresponding Italics.[37]

170 pt

JuS

1

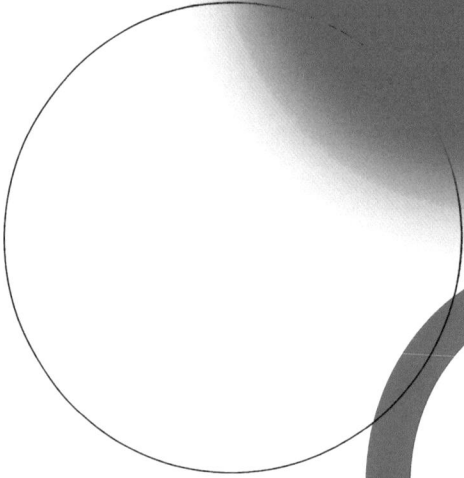

2

3

8 pt	Thight monospace type
9 pt	Thight monospace type
10 pt	Thight monospace type
11 pt	Thight monospace type
12 pt	Thight monospace type
14 pt	Thight monospace type
18 pt	Thight monospace type
24 pt	Thight monospace type
30pt	Thight monospace
36 pt	Thight monospac
48 pt	Thight mono
60 pt	Thight mo
72 pt	Thight

Vulf Mono

abcdefghijklmnopqrstuvwxyz

ABCDEFGHIJKLMNOPQRSTUVWXYZ

1234567890

Designer	
	James Edmondson

Foundry	
	OH no Type

Release	
	2019

World Wide Web	

About

Vulf Mono is the official typeface of Vulfpeck, a funky four piece rhythm section from Ann Arbor, Michigan. The typeface draws its main inspiration from 12 Point Light Italic, a font for the IBM Selectric typewriter.[38]

189 pt

hM

MonoLisa

abcdefghijklmnopqrstuvwxyz

Uppercase

ABCDEFGHIJKLMNOPQRSTUVWXYZ

Punctuation

.,:;- – — _!?¡…•·*+'""' `´ ‹«»›

Symbols

§©®™¶£@&⇧⇨⇪⌧⏎⏏⏚⏛⏻∣☾∞☐▲▼☼◑◐◗◕◔☽◪◸◹◺⬓◻⬛⬜☠☺☹☾☀♥❄➔⚡☑⌧

Figures

1234567890

Designer	Marcus Sterz
Foundry	FaceType Foundry
Release	2020
World Wide Web	

170 pt

AgC

```java
/**
 *
 * <p>
 *
 * @author unseen
 *a
 * @since 1.0.0
 */
public final class MonospaceTypefaceCollection
{
    /**
     * <p>
     * Coding fonts or not
     * </p>
     * @param font
     *                Font
     *
     * @return TRUE: This is a font for coding FALSE: This is not a
font for coding
     *
     *  @see ProgrammingFontManager.Font
     * /
    public state boolean isCodingFont(int Font)
    {
        String[] strings = new String[]{`1234567890`,
                                        `abcdefghijklmnopqrstuvwxyz`
                                        `ABCDEFGHIJKLMNOPQRSTUVWYZ`};

        System.out.println(strings);
        return true;

}
```

As software developers, we always strive for better tools but rarely consider font as such. Yet we spend most of our days looking at screens reading and writing code. Using a wrong font can negatively impact our productivity and lead to bugs. "MonoLisa" was designed by professionals to improve developers' productivity and reduce fatigue.

Designing a monospace font is much harder than a traditional, proportional one: being constrained by the same width of all glyphs can result in a boring or unreadable font.

Choosing a typeface is a like choosing your laptop, your editor, or any other developer tool. It's a subtle but important choice given you end up using it a lot.

Spending most of our days reading and writing code can be tiring, especially on our eyes, affecting our ability to concentrate and may lead to bugs in our software.[39]

Marcus Sterz, Juho Vepsäläinen, Andrey Okonetchnikov

Marcus Sterz, font and graphic designer, worked with software developers Andrey Okonetchnikov and Juho Vepsäläinen to create the ideal typeface for coding.

What prompted you to design a coding typeface?
Was it the first time for you designing a
coding font? And have you been involved with
coding before?

I was looking for a new project, then I had an interesting conversation. *MonoLisa* may not be my first monospaced typeface, but it is the first serious one, even where it really made sense, instead of just being formalism. Before that, it was more of a display gimmick. And no, coding was not an issue for me before, I still cannot program a single line of text.

How did the idea for "MonoLisa" came about?
What story stands behind it?

In the beginning there was a conversation with two programmers who had their places in my shared office at the time. Andrey Okonetchnikov and Juho Vepsäläinen. Both are very experienced programmers and when we chatted about coding fonts I realized how immensely important good fonts are in this area and how little choice there is. Programmers look at lines of code for several hours a day and cannot really afford to work with bad fonts. By "bad" I mean: difficult to read, unbalanced, unclear design language ...

How far did Andrey Okonetchnikov and Juho
Vepsäläinen contribute to the creation of
"MonoLisa?" Can you give an insight into the
development process of "MonoLisa?"

Their input was immensely important as they have a lot of insight into the scene and even give lectures, workshops and even conferences within the coding scene. They know what coders need because they are deeply rooted in the scene. That also helped with marketing: *MonoLisa* is currently only available through a single website, but we have already won many customers who are happy about every update. Programmers are a much more active group of buyers than customers at Myfonts, for example. They help us with problem solving on our feedback channel Github. With the usual desktop fonts, I only sent an update when I or a customer came across a bug, otherwise the process was actually completed with the publication. It's different with *MonoLisa:* we want to make it the golden standard of coding fonts, and we are constantly expanding and optimizing *MonoLisa.* A free update is published every few weeks and we document it: new characters, new languages, new ligatures ...

What defines a "good" font for programming?
And how do you judge the legibility of
non-proportional typefaces?

> Monospace typefaces have a systemic problem: the mono-space. Balancing the space is very important here. It can't actually be perfect, but I think we have presented a very good candidate with *MonoLisa*. It was also important to me to design letters constructed similarly, such as (G / C, I / l / 1 ... — you can see this at monolisa.dev — so differently that no "reading out" is possible. Reading out means wasting time and frustration.
>
> What many other designers do, what I think is the wrong way: One should not construct monospaced typefaces "tech-noid," such as *Jetbrains Mono*, because they already have a technology-based limitation. I understand the temptation to emphasize the technical, because that is also fascinating, but it is extremely detrimental to readability. You have to design it organically, because it's about legibility, not geometry.

And a short question at the very end:
Do you have a favorite monospaced font in
addition to "MonoLisa?"

> *Fira Code* is one of our main competitors in terms of con-tent and target group. I find *Operator Mono* from Hoefler & Co interesting, also a very organically designed monospace, although the code text may seem a little too shaky. *IBM Plex* is very beautiful, with a very suitable and cleverly designed microsite.

Find out more about "MonoLisa" on monolisa.dev

SYNO MONO

Lowercase

Uppercase

Punctuation

. . . —

Figures

Designer

Release ⊠◖⊠◖ (2020)

World Wide Web

About   *SYNO MONO* was initially created for the Human Machine Interface
          microsite promoting his debut album *Futurspective.* Further explora-
          tions led to three different styles inspired by the synopsis of human and
          machine.[40]

174 pt

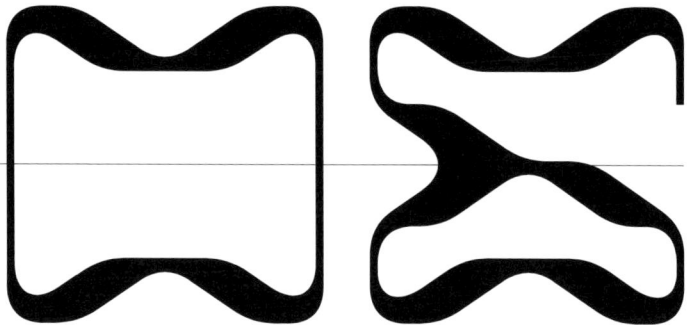

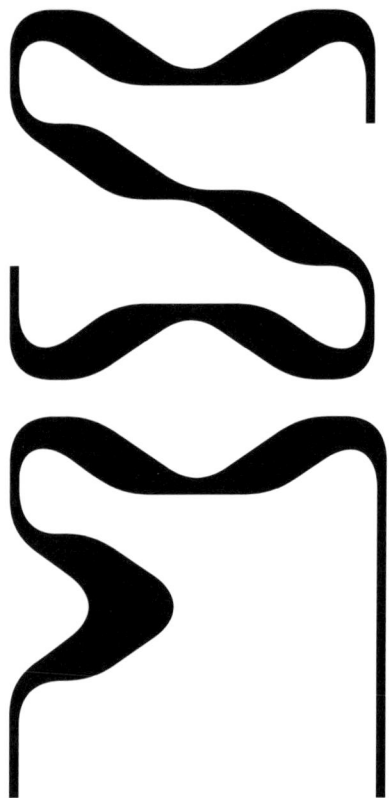

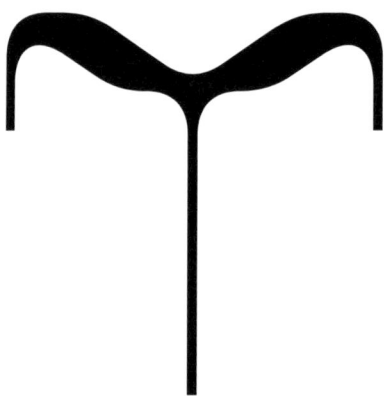

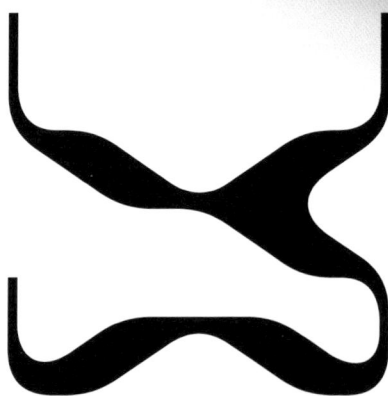

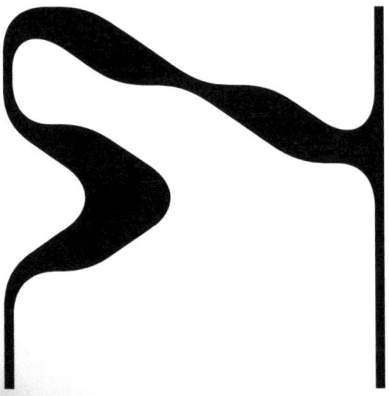

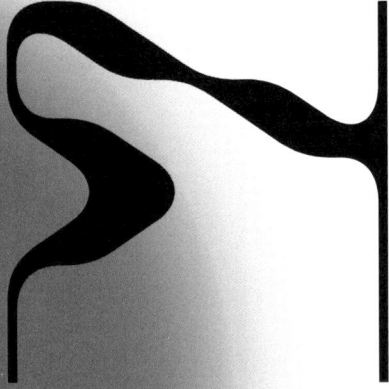

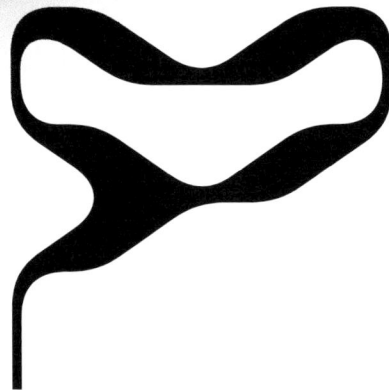
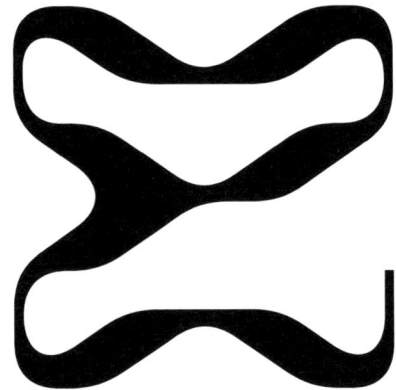

Typist Slab

Lowercase	abcdefghijklmnopqrstuvwxyz

Uppercase	ABCDEFGHIJKLMNOPQRSTUVWXYZ

Punctuation	. , : ; - – — _ ! ? ¡ .... · * + ' " " ' ˇ ‹ « »

Symbols	ß©® £@&

Ligatures	ij

Figures	1234567890

Designer	Nicolien van der Keur

Foundry	VanderKeur

Release	2020

World Wide Web	

About	A typeface inspired by the design of typefaces used on early developed typewriters. A characteristic of this style is the spherical ends of a number of glyphs. *Typist Slab* is a monospaced typeface available in six weights.[41]

152 pt

GsR

Typist Code

Lowercase

abcdefghijklmnopqrstuvwxyz

Uppercase

ABCDEFGHIJKLMNOPQRSTUVWXYZ

Punctuation

. , : ; - – — _ ! ? ¡ .... · * + ' " " ' ˇ ‹ « » ›

Symbols

§©® £@&

Ligatures

ij

Figures

1234567890

Designer	Nicolien van der Keur
Foundry	VanderKeur
Release	2020
World Wide Web	

About
A typeface for programmers when to are coding. A characteristic of this style is the half spherical ends of a number of glyphs. *Typist Code* is a monospaced typeface available in six weights and fits perfectly next to *Typist Slab*.[42]

170 pt

QcZ

Design of Typist

The typeface *Typist* originated during an extensive research on the origin and development of typewriter type styles. The first commercially manufactured typewriter came on the market in 1878 by Remington. The type styles on these machines were only possible in capitals, the combination of capitals and lowercase came available around the end of the nineteenth century. Apart from a few exceptions, most type styles had a fixed letter width and a more or less unambiguous design that resembled a thread-like structure. A lot of this mechanical structure was due to the method the type styles were produced.

It is our duty to correct the errors of books, and to make sense of defective passages. But the incompetent author who is afflicted with a desire to write makes a compilation without sagacity and piles up fault on fault; he covers paper with blots and scratc es, and disfigures his copy. He does not spend nine years on his work; he takes no pains to amend or polish it; but he makes

Figure 1: Engravers Hairline No. 644.
Bruce's Type Foundry, 1853.
New York: George Bruce's Son & Co.

ABCDEFGHIJK
LMNOPQRSTU
VWXYZÆŒ!&

Figure 2: Long-Primer Engravers Hairline.
Bruce's Type Foundry, 1882.
New York: George Bruce's Son & Co.

abcdefghijklmnopqrstuvwxyz
ABCDEFGHIJKLMNOPQRSTUVWXYZ
$123456789. (Mr.) "N" Nº
Type-Writer No. 59 1879

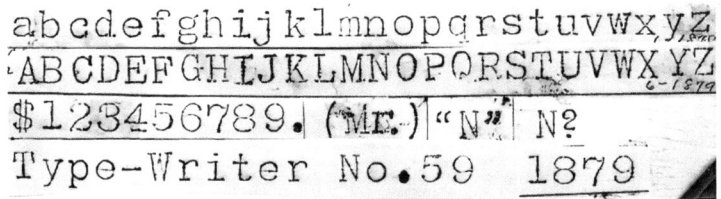

Figure 3: Type test from Model Nr. 59
of a Remington Typewriter from 1879
Courtesy of Peter V. Tytell from New York.

Looking at type specimens for print before the first type-writers were good enough to came on the market we can see that in 1853 (Figure 1) and in 1882 (Figure 2) Bruce's Type Foundry already had printing type that had a structure of the typewriter type styles. Of course printing types were proportional designed as typewriter type styles had a fixed width (Figure 3). So it is possible that except from the method of production for typewriter type styles, the design of printing types were copied.

In the design of the *Typist,* the purpose was — next to the monospace feature — to include some of the features of the early typewriter type styles. Features such as the ball terminals and the remarkable design of the letter "Q."

This new typeface laks the mechanical and cold look of the early typewriter type styles. The *Typist* comes in six weights with matching italics in two versions. One that resembled the early typewriter type styles (*Typist Slab*) and a version designed with coding programmers in mind (*Typist Code*).

Nicolien van der Keur

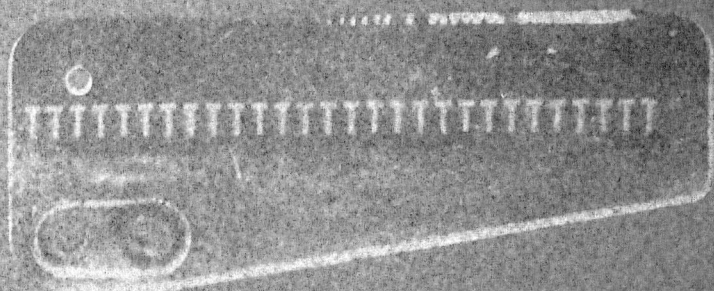

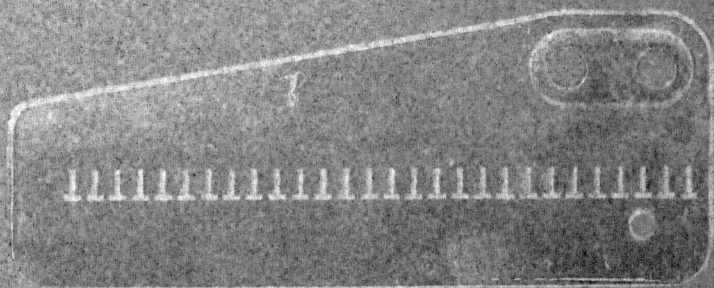

Index

Index

A   Airport Mono   2014–2017

→ P. 114–117   Piero Di Biase

Andalé Mono   1997

→ P. 36–37   Steve Matteson

Anonymus Pro   2009

→ P. 56–59   Mark Simonson

AO Mono

→ P. 24–27   Atelier Olschinsky

Aperçu Mono   2010

→ P. 74–77   The Entente

Atlas Typewriter   2012
Susana Carvalho
Kai Bernau
→ P. 90–93   Ilya Ruderman

B   Base Mono   1997

→ P. 38–41   Zuzana Licko

Basier Mono   2019

→ P. 158–161

Index

	Blue Mono	2012
	→ P. 94–97	Jérémie Nuel
C	Calico Mono Ink Trapped	2010
	→ P. 78–81	Mirage Design Studio
	Cindie D	2016
	→ P. 118–121	Lewis McGuffie
	Consolas	2007
	→ P. 52–55	Lucas de Groot
	Courier	1955
	→ P. 12–15	Howard Kettler
	Cygnito Mono	2019
	→ P. 162–165	Radinal Riki
D	Droulers	2017 Julia Joffre Yoann Minet
	→ P. 132–135	Camille Prandi
E	Eureka Mono	2010
	→ P. 44–47	Peter Bil'ak

Index

G   **GT Pressura Mono**

2012–2017

→ P. 106–109

Marc Kappeler
Dominik Huber

I   **IBM Plex Mono**

2017
Mike Abbink
Paul van der Laan

→ P. 136–139

Pieter van Rosmalen

Input Mono

2016

→ P. 110–113

David Jonathan Ross

K   **Kettler**

2002

→ P. 48–51

Eric Olsen

L   **Letter Gothic**

1962

→ P. 20–23

Roger Roberson

LTC Remington Typewriter

2018
Lanston Type Company
Frederic Goudy

→ P. 140–143

Paul D. Hunt

M   **Maison Mono**

2010

→ P. 82–85

Timo Gaessner

Monaco

2009

→ P. 60–63

Kris Holmes
Susan Kare

Index

Monoela
→ P. 122–127

2016

André Leonhardt
Dennis Michaelis

MonoLisa
→ P. 172–179

2020

Marcus Sterz

Monument Grotesk Mono
→ P. 144–149

2018

Kasper-Florio
Dinamo

O **Orator**
→ P. 26–29

1962

John Scheppler

P **Pica 10 Pitch**
→ P. 16–19

1990

IBM

Pitch
→ P. 98–101

2012

Kris Sowersby

Plastic
→ P. 150–153

2018

Jitka Janečková
Ivana Palečková

Platelet
→ P. 30–33

1993

Conor Mangat

Index

R **Roboto Mono** — 2012
→ P. 102–103 — Christian Robertson

S **Simon Mono Light** — 2018
→ P. 146–149 — JP Haynie / Robert Janes

Sneak Mono — 2019
→ P. 166–169 — Fabian Fohrer

Source Code Pro — 2012
→ P. 104–105 — Paul D. Hunt

Space Mono — 2016
→ P. 128–131 — Colophon Foundry

Splendid 66
→ P. 64–65 — Johan Holmdahl

Sudo — 2009
→ P. 66–69 — Jens Kutílek

Suisse Int'l Mono — 2011
→ P. 88–89 — Ian Party / Swiss Typefaces

	SYNO MONO	2020
	→ P. 180–183	Lukas Haider
T	**The Future Mono**	2018
	→ P. 154–157	Kris Sowersby Noe Blanco
	TheSans Mono	1994
	→ P. 34–35	Lucas de Groot
	Typist Code	2020
	→ P. 186–189	Nicolien van der Keur
	Typist Slab	2020
	→ P. 183–185 → P. 188–189	Nicolien van der Keur
U	**Ubuntu Mono**	2010
	→ P. 86–87	Dalton Maag
V	**Vulf Mono**	2019
	→ P. 170–171	James Edmondson

Appendix

Picture

All pictures
                in this book
have been taken
by Christina Wunderlich.

Credits

Source: World wide web
Date: 06-25-2020

1   fontsinuse.com/typefaces/69/
    courier?filters
    =blog-posts-only&order=most-
    viewed

2   fontshop.com/people/noah-
    nazir/fontlists/
    letter-gothic-alternatives-1

3   fonts.com/de/font/linotype/
    orator/story

4   fonts.adobe.com/fonts

5   platelet/details/n4

6   lucasfonts.com/fonts/
    the-sans/info

7   typewolf.com/site-of-the-
    day/fonts/andale-
    mono

8   emigre.com/PDF/BaseMono.pdf

9   fontshop.com/people/
    fontshop-team/fontlists/
    symbol-arrows

10 processtypefoundry.com/
    fonts/kettler

11 lucasfonts.com/fonts/
    consolas/info

12 marksimonson.com/fonts/view/
    anonymous-pro

13 kutilek.de/sudo-font

14 colophon-foundry.org/
    typefaces/apercu

15 milieugrotesque.com/
    specimen/maison

16 design.ubuntu.com/font

17 swisstypefaces.com/fonts/
    suisse/#font

18 commercialtype.com/catalog/
    atlas_typewriter

19 volcano-type.de/fonts/
    categories/display/bl
    ue_not_mono/blue_mono.com

20 klim.co.nz/retail-fonts/
    pitch

21 fonts.google.com/specimen/
    Roboto+Mono

22 fonts.google.com/specimen/
    Source+Code+Pro

23 grillitype.com/typeface/
    gt-pressura

24 djr.com/input

25 t-wo.it/font/airport-mono

26 lewismcguffie.com/Cindie-
    Mono-Typeface-1

27 colophon-foundry.org/custom/
    spacemono

28 bureaubrut.com/en/product/
    droulers

29 ibm.com/plex

30 ibm.com/plex

31 p22.com/family-Remington_
    Typewriter

32 abcdinamo.com/typefaces/
    monument-grotesk

33 abcdinamo.com/standards
    plastic-typeface.com

34 futurefonts.xyz/klim/
    the-future-mono

35 atipofoundry.com/fonts/
    basier-mono

36 ywft.us/29f00a93e

37 tightype.com/typefaces/sneak

38 ohnotype.co/fonts/vulf

39 monolisa.dev

40 lukashaider.com/Type

41 vanderkeur.net/typist-
    typeface

42 vanderkeur.net/typist-
    typeface

Position Monospace —
Nichtproportionale Schriften
gestern, heute, morgen

Robert Steinmüller

For more background information on the subject of non-proportional typefaces regards to their origin, use, classification, and future use based on their history, have a look at Robert Steinmüllers's research based master's thesis. The focus was set on examining the design development and aesthetics of these typefaces — in contrast to direct a typeface analysis. Complemented by interviews with type designers and designers, the current position of monospace is worked out in this book.

robertsteinmueller.de

Language: German
Planned to be published

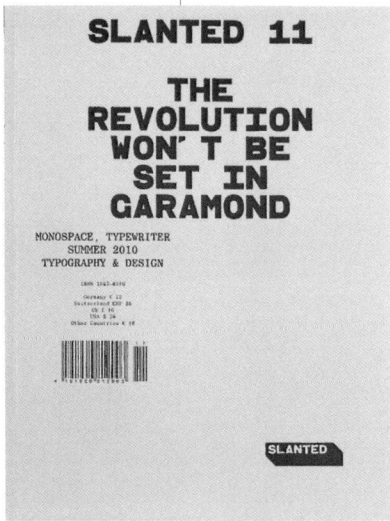

SLANTED 11

THE
REVOLUTION
WON'T BE
SET IN
GARAMOND

MONOSPACE, TYPEWRITER
SUMMER 2010
TYPOGRAPHY & DESIGN

SLANTED

Slanted Magazine #11:
Monospace, Typewriter

The Revolution won't be set
in Garamond

"The Revolution won't be set in Garamond" — comes in revised structure and
layout. Projects are confronted with
each other, magazine sections over-
lap. The changes reflect our attitude
towards contemporary editorial design
in analog and digital times. This "new
order" is a homage to the visual and to
design. Orientation, information, and
sections still have their own right and
place within the magazine's structure,
but the changing of perspectives, the
relations, and associations are defi-
nitely not an expression by the medium
of information, rather of openness
and examination. It's a concept that
doesn't come under the hegemony of
function, a feast of the visual.

slanted.de

Language: English, German
Release: August 2010

Imprint

Slanted Publishers UG
(haftungsbeschränkt)
Nebeniusstrasse 10
76137 Karlsruhe
Germany
T +49 (0) 721 85148268
info@slanted.de
slanted.de
@slanted_publishers

© Slanted Publishers, Karlsruhe, 2022
Nebeniusstraße 10, 76137 Karlsruhe, Germany
© Design and Concept by Christina Wunderlich, 2022

ISBN: 978-3-948440-32-9

Design:	Christina Wunderlich
	servus@christinawunderlich.de
	christinawunderlich.de
Publishing Direction:	Lars Harmsen, Julia Kahl
Production Management:	Clara Weinreich
Supervision:	Prof. Jürgen Huber, Torsten Köchlin
Proofreading:	Clara Weinreich, Julia Kahl
Printing:	Gilch GmbH
Paper Cover:	EXTRASMOOTH Coldwhite 350 g/sm
Paper Inside:	SMOOTH White 120 g/sm
	by Metapaper
Typefaces:	Droulers, Monument Grotesk Regular / Italic
	Monument Grotesk Mono, Monument Grotesk Semi-Mono
Other Typefaces:	Airport Mono, Andalé Mono, Anonymus Pro, AO Mono,
	Aperçu Mono, Atlas Typewriter, Base Mono, Basier
	Mono, Blue Mono, Calico Mono , Cindie D, Consolas,
	Courier, Cygnito Mono, Eureka Mono, GT Pressura Mono,
	IBM Plex Mono, Input Mono, Kettler, Letter Gothic,
	LTC Remington, Maison Mono, Monaco, Monoela, MonoLisa,
	Orator, Pica 10 Pitch, Pitch, Plastic, Platelet,
	Roboto Mono, Simon Mono Light, Sneak Mono, Source Code
	Pro, Space Mono, Splendid 66, Sudo, Suisse Int'l Mono,
	SYNO MONO, The Future Mono, TheSans Mono, Typist Code,
	Typist Slab, Ubuntu Mono, Vulf Mono

Imprint

About

Slanted Publishers is an internationally active independent publishing and media house, founded in 2014 by Lars Harmsen and Julia Kahl. They publish the award-winning print magazine Slanted, which twice a year focuses on international design and culture. The Slanted blog www.slanted.de and social media have been publishing daily news, events, and inspiring portfolios from around the world ever since. In addition to the Slanted blog and magazine, Slanted Publishers initiates and creates projects such as the Yearbook of Type, tear-off calendars Typodarium and Photodarium, independent type foundry VolcanoType and others. Slanted's publishing program reflects their own diverse interests, focusing on contempo-rary design and culture, working closely with editors and authors to produce outstanding publications with meaningful content and high quality. These publications can be found in the Slanted Shop alongside other extraordinary products by young design talents and established producers from all over the world. Slanted was born from great passion and has made a name for itself across the globe. Its design is vibrant and inspiring — its philosophy open-minded, tolerant, and curious.

Thank You

I would like to extend a big thank you to all the designers providing their typefaces and supporting this project.

Special Thanks to Dinamo Typefaces providing their typeface "Monument Grotesk."

I would particularly like to thank María Ramos, Horst Wöhrle, Dennis Michaelis, André Leonhardt, and Marcus Sterz for their contributions.